GET JUICED!

EASY JUICE RECIPES PACKED WITH NUTRITIOUS SUPER FOODS

pil

Publications International, Ltd.

Let's get social!

🅾 @Publications_International

🅵 @PublicationsInternational

www.pilcookbooks.com

CONTENTS

JUICING 101

RAISE A GLASS TO YOUR HEALTH

If your idea of juice is limited to that little glass of OJ next to your breakfast plate, you're in for a delicious, nutritious surprise. You can enjoy juices from a cornucopia of colorful, flavorful fruits and vegetables using an electric juicer and the simple recipes and tips in this book. As you'll quickly discover, juicing is an easy and convenient way to fit more fresh produce into your daily diet. And that's a proven path to better health and a lower risk of disease.

WHY START JUICING?

We've all heard the news—from doctors, nutritionists, the media and even the U.S. government: We need to eat more fruits and vegetables. These gifts from the garden (and orchard) are naturally rich sources of many of the vitamins and minerals that are essential to life. But more than that, research has shown time and again that getting plenty of fruits and vegetables can help us function at our best and protect us from a host of health problems, including heart disease and certain cancers. Scientists suspect these benefits come from the unique combinations of nutrients—including vitamins, minerals and special plant chemicals called phytonutrients—that are naturally present in produce. Studies using supplements of the most promising individual nutrients just don't produce the same health rewards.

With so much to gain, it just makes good sense to give fruits and vegetables a major place in our daily meals. Indeed, many experts say we should aim to fill half of our plate with fruits and vegetables at every meal. And the greater the variety of produce we choose, the more likely we are to cover our nutritional bases and gain the widest protection against everyday ills and chronic diseases.

Sadly, most of us don't come close to getting the minimum 2 cups of fruits and 2½ cups of vegetables a day that are recommended in the government's latest Dietary Guidelines for Americans. If you're one of those people—if you struggle to get the amount or variety of produce that your body deserves on a daily basis—juicing can help you bridge the gap. Juicing is also a great way to give yourself some additional, natural "health insurance."

You might think all juices are good for you, but seemingly healthy options can sometimes be deceiving. That fruity juice drink, for example, may actually contain less than 10 percent actual juice from fruit—and not necessarily from the fruit touted on the label. The rest of the carton or bottle may be filled with little more than artificial flavoring, artificial coloring and sugar water. But when you have a juicer, you can quickly turn fresh fruits and vegetables into delicious, invigorating juices that retain a high percentage of the original produce's vitamins, minerals and phytonutrients. Plus, you can control what goes into the machine, so you can be sure the resulting juices aren't loaded with sugar, salt or other additives that you don't need or want.

Using a juicer also makes exploring new produce options very simple. Preparing most fruits and vegetables for juicing often involves little more than washing the produce and feeding it into your juicer. The recipes in this book show you how to use more than 60 kinds of produce to create some truly delicious juices. In the process of trying those recipes, you're sure to come across plenty of fruits and vegetables that you'll want to start adding to your plate as well as your juicer.

But what if you (or other members of your household) simply aren't that into fruits or, more commonly, vegetables? What if your fork rarely strays beyond vegetable standbys like corn, potatoes and iceberg lettuce—unless, of course, there's plenty of fatty cheese, butter, gravy or dressing on hand? What if the closest you typically come to a serving of fruit is a slice of watermelon in the summer, a smear of strawberry jelly on your toast or the bananas in your banana split?

Truthfully, juicing alone can't make up for an overall poor diet. Even if you create and enjoy juice from a variety of produce each day, you still need to make the effort to include as many whole fruits and vegetables into your daily menu as possible. Your health depends on it. Because even though most of the vitamins, minerals and phytonutrients from the whole produce make it into the freshly made juice, the fiber does not. And that fiber contributes to many of the healing effects associated with fruits and vegetables.

Still, juicing can be a valuable part of a healthy diet. It can help fill the gaps when your produce intake falls short and provide your body with extra doses of disease-fighting nutrients. You can use it as an easy way to sample a wide variety of fruits and vegetables. You may even find yourself drinking juices made with vegetables you're not fond of because they've been combined with other fruits or vegetables that you do like. And that's far healthier than using a thick coating of cheese or gravy to make a food more appealing.

TYPES OF JUICERS

Some of juicing's growing popularity is due to advances in juicing technology. While an old-fashioned citrus juicer can turn out a fine glass of orange or grapefruit juice, the latest high-powered electric juice extractors can quickly juice a gamut of fruits and vegetables—from apples and asparagus to watermelon and zucchini. They also tend to be fairly easy to operate and are available in a range of models to fit most budgets.

The electric juice extractors that can handle a wide range of produce come in two main types: masticating (also known as cold press because they do not produce heat as they extract the juice) and centrifugal. A masticating juicer works by smashing fruits and vegetables, much as our teeth crush food, and then using intense pressure to squeeze out the juice. Masticating juicers are quieter and tend to extract more juice from the pulp than do centrifugal juicers. But masticating juicers also tend to be heavier, bulkier and more expensive than centrifugal juicers.

In a centrifugal juicer, a sharp, rotating metal blade or shredding disk grates the fruits and vegetables, and as the pieces spin around in a mesh basket, centrifugal force separates the juice from the pulp. Some centrifugal juicers have an automatic pulp ejector that sends the pulp into a side container once the juice has been extracted from it; this feature helps to make cleanup quicker and easier. Another useful feature available on some centrifugal juicers is an extra-wide mouth that allows you to feed larger pieces of fruits or vegetables (sometimes even whole fruits) into the machine, thus reducing or eliminating time spent cutting up produce for the juicer.

Compared to masticating juicers, centrifugal juicers tend to be somewhat faster, easier to operate and clean, more affordable and more widely available. They are also more popular. For these reasons, the information and recipes in this book were developed with the centrifugal type of juicer in mind.

USING AND CARING FOR YOUR JUICER

Using your juicer correctly and taking proper care of it will help to extend its life, prevent problems with the machine and ensure that you get the greatest amount and quality of juice from it. The following tips can make doing so easier.

- Before you use your juicer for the first time, be sure to thoroughly read the manual supplied by the manufacturer. This can't be emphasized enough. While the information in this book generally applies to centrifugal juicers, it's important for you to read and follow the specific instructions, warnings and recommendations in the manual provided by the manufacturer of your machine. Not doing so may result in injury to you, damage to the machine, less than optimal juicing results and/or voiding of any warranties on the juicer. Once you begin using your machine, keep the manual handy for quick reference. It often contains helpful tips on preparing different types of produce for the best results.

- Be sure to use your juicer on a solid surface that's clean, dry and level. Position it well away from the edge of the surface so that vibration or an accidental nudge does not send it tumbling to the floor.

- Use extreme caution in handling any blades or other sharp parts when assembling, disassembling or cleaning your juicer.

- If your juicer comes with a tool for pushing fruits and vegetables into the machine, use it whenever you add produce to your machine; do not use your fingers or a kitchen tool instead. Press firmly but slowly on the pusher to maximize the amount of juice extracted.

- Before juicing hard fruits or vegetables, check the manual to determine if the machine needs to be stopped at intervals to prevent excess strain on the motor.

- To help keep pulp from clogging machine parts, alternate soft and hard produce whenever possible.

- Do not pour liquid or extremely soft ingredients—such as water, juice, yogurt or applesauce—into the juicer unless the manual states that you may do so.

- Be diligent about thoroughly cleaning your juicer after each use. Carefully following the manufacturer's cleaning instructions will not only help to keep the juicer in good working order, it can help protect you from food poisoning caused by the growth of harmful bacteria on the machine's parts.

- Be sure the unit is turned off and unplugged before disassembling and/or cleaning the machine.

- Never submerge the base unit (containing the motor) in water. Follow the instructions in the manual, which typically call for wiping down the unit with a damp soft cloth or nonabrasive sponge.

- Remove and wash the detachable parts of the juicer immediately after use, or at least rinse or soak them to help keep pulp from drying on the surfaces.

- Parts of the juicer that are dishwasher safe (check the manual) should typically be placed on the top shelf only.

- To make cleanup quicker and easier, use a disposable plastic produce bag to line your juicer's pulp-collection container (unless the manual directs otherwise). Once you've finished juicing, simply lift the bag out of the pulp container and discard the pulp, set it aside for use in other recipes, or add it to your garden or compost pile.

- If brightly colored fruits or vegetables (such as berries or beets) have left stains on washable plastic parts of your machine, try soaking the parts in water to which you've added a small amount of lemon juice.

TIPS FOR BETTER JUICING

The following tips can help improve your juicing experience:

- Use the freshest fruits and vegetables to obtain the best tasting and most nutritious juice.

- Make only as much juice as you need right away. With no preservatives, fresh juice begins to lose flavor and nutrients immediately after juicing.

- For best results, select produce that is ripe (or if necessary, nearly ripe) and still on the firm side. Softer pieces do not do as well in centrifugal juicers.

- Wash your hands with soap and warm water immediately prior to working with produce or any other food.

- Always wash all fruits and vegetables thoroughly—even those you intend to peel—before juicing them. Otherwise, debris and bacteria from the surface can be transferred to the flesh within when you cut into or handle it. Use a vegetable brush or other clean, firm-bristled brush, if necessary, to remove embedded dirt.

- Wash and, if necessary, cut, peel or otherwise prepare produce just before putting it into the juicer.

- Cut out any bruised, soft or damaged areas from produce before putting it into the juicer.

- If you're using produce that has a hard, waxy or inedible skin or rind, peel it before juicing. (The individual ingredient profiles that follow indicate when this is necessary or recommended.)

- Large or hard pits, stones or seeds should be removed from produce before it is fed into the juicer.

- When a recipe calls for leafy greens or fresh herbs, try sandwiching them between pieces of more substantial produce or rolling them up into a tight ball before feeding them into the juicer.

- If the flavor of a juice is too intense, try adding more mildly flavored fruits or vegetables or those with a higher water content (celery, for example) to the mix the next time you make it. Doing so should help dilute the overpowering taste.

Once you've made at least some of the recipes in this book and feel more comfortable with the whole juicing process, try doing some experimenting to create your own personalized juice combinations. After all, variety is the spice of life!

GREAT JUICING INGREDIENTS

The following profiles highlight many of the best and most nutritious options for juicing. In each profile, you'll find information on the ingredient's major nutrients and potential health benefits as well as advice on preparing it for the juicer. The profiles are in alphabetical order for convenient reference. Following the profiles, you'll find an assortment of delectable juice recipes. Enjoy!

APPLES

Benefits: Science has given us evidence to support the old adage that "an apple a day keeps the doctor away." Apples and their fresh juice are rich in vitamin C, which is essential to a strong immune system. Frequently including apples into your juice blends may be one of the best things you can do to help your body fight off colds, flu and other illnesses. Apples also contain vitamins A, E and K and the minerals potassium and calcium.

Preparation: Wash apples under cool running water and twist off the stems. If your juicer can handle their size, feed whole apples, unpeeled, into the machine. If not, cut into halves or quarters.

APRICOTS

Benefits: Apricots are a great source of beta-carotene, a form of vitamin A that also acts as a powerful antioxidant, meaning that it helps protect cells in the body from damage caused by exposure to unstable oxygen molecules. In addition, the vitamin A activity of beta-carotene helps to protect eyesight. Apricots also offer potassium—which helps the body regulate blood pressure—as well as some calcium and iron.

Preparation: Wash apricots gently but thoroughly in cool running water. Cut the fruit in half and remove the pits.

ASPARAGUS

Benefits: Asparagus can help shield your heart and blood vessels from damage. It provides potassium, a mineral essential for balancing out the sodium in our diets and keeping blood pressure under control. The tall, slender spears also offer two antioxidant vitamins—A, in the form of beta-carotene, and C—that studies suggest can aid in the fight against heart disease.

Preparation: Rinse individual spears thoroughly, use the side of a knife blade or a vegetable peeler to scrape off the tough skin on the lower part of each stalk (the section you'd remove and discard prior to cooking) and trim off any dried-out ends.

BASIL

Benefits: The magnesium in basil can improve blood flow throughout the body by causing blood vessels to relax, a benefit for people who suffer from high blood pressure or hardening of the arteries. Fresh basil also contributes beta-carotene and phytonutrients called flavonoids that are part of the body's natural defenses against damage caused by oxygen—damage that is thought to lead to multiple diseases, including cancer and heart disease.

Preparation: Wash basil thoroughly by swishing it in a bowl of cold water and blotting dry with a paper towel. Roll the sprigs into a ball or sandwich them between more substantial produce, then feed into the juicer.

BEETS

Benefits: Beets are a great source of folic acid, an essential B vitamin that's especially valuable for women of childbearing age because it can help prevent neural-tube birth defects in their offspring. Beets also contain vitamin C, which actually helps to preserve folic acid in addition to being important for a strong immune system. And beets provide potassium, which is important for controlling blood pressure.

Preparation: Wash beets gently to prevent breaks in the skin that will allow the color and nutrients to escape. If you must cut up the beets to fit them in the juicer, consider wearing rubber gloves and an apron to prevent staining your hands and clothes.

BELL PEPPERS

Benefits: Bell peppers contain more vitamin C than citrus fruits; they also offer a rich store of vitamin A in the form of beta-carotene. Together, these antioxidant nutrients may help defend the body's cells and tissues from damage that can lead to a host of health problems which become more common as we age, such as heart attack, stroke and certain cancers. Bell peppers also contain a phytonutrient called lutein, which may help reduce the risk of the sight-stealing disease macular degeneration.

Preparation: Wash peppers thoroughly under cool running water. Remove the stems and as many seeds as you can and cut into two or three pieces.

BLACKBERRIES

Benefits: The deep, dark color of blackberries results from high levels of anthocyanins, a type of antioxidant phytonutrient that works to defend the body's cells against free radicals (unstable oxygen molecules). Free radical damage contributes to many negative effects, from cataracts and cancerous cells to wrinkles and age spots. Blackberries are also rich in vitamin C and a phytonutrient called ellagic acid, both potent cancer fighters in their own right.

Preparation: Wash berries gently but thoroughly under cool running water.

BLUEBERRIES

Benefits: Blueberries have one of the highest antioxidant contents of any fruit, and those antioxidants appear useful in warding off heart attack, stroke and certain cancers. Some research even suggests that the antioxidant power of blueberries may help protect brain cells and cognitive function and possibly even partially reverse some early memory loss among older adults. Blueberries also supply both iron and vitamin C, a beneficial combination since vitamin C enables the body to better absorb iron from plant foods. And like their cousins the cranberries, blueberries can help prevent and treat urinary tract infections.

Preparation: Wash berries gently but thoroughly under cool running water.

BOK CHOY

Benefits: Bok choy's deep green hue advertises its hefty beta-carotene load, meaning it can help the body protect itself from disease-causing damage. This cabbage variety also offers potassium and calcium, minerals that help the body regulate blood pressure. And unlike other nondairy calcium sources, bok choy is low in oxalates, a substance that decreases calcium absorption. Adequate calcium intake is vital for maintaining strong bones and teeth.

Preparation: Remove any cut or browning leaves, then use a sharp knife to cut off the bottom of the plant so the stalks separate. Rinse dirt from individual stalks and leaves under cool running water.

BROCCOLI

Benefits: Broccoli is a treasure trove of valuable nutrients, including vitamins C, E and A (mostly as the antioxidant beta-carotene) and minerals such as calcium, folate and potassium. The vitamin C and beta-carotene help shield the body's cells from everyday damage that can lead to disease. The vitamin E not only helps defend the body's tissues but protects other antioxidants. Calcium is important for strong bones throughout life, folate helps prevent certain birth defects and potassium plays a role in warding off stroke.

Preparation: Remove and discard the large woody stem and cut the head into pieces that will fit in the juicer. Rinse the pieces thoroughly under cool running water.

BRUSSELS SPROUTS

Benefits: Brussels sprouts are a good source of protein compared to most other fruits and vegetables, and they're far lower in calories and sodium than animal sources of protein. The vegetable protein is not complete, but it is an essential component of countless body tissues—including your muscles, organs, skin and even hair and nails. Brussels sprouts are also packed with potent phytonutrients and vitamin C, which help protect your body from damage and disease.

Preparation: Rinse Brussels sprouts under cool running water, pull off wilted leaves and trim the stem ends.

BUTTERNUT SQUASH

Benefits: The orange-yellow color of this squash shouts beta-carotene, that antioxidant precursor of vitamin A that works to defend the body's tissues from damage caused by exposure to sunlight, toxic fumes, radiation, tobacco smoke and other potentially cancer-causing substances. It also provides decent amounts of vitamin C for a healthy immune system and calcium for strong bones.

Preparation: Use a sharp knife or vegetable peeler to remove the peel, then cut the squash in half lengthwise. Scoop out the seeds and pulp, lay the halves flat side down and cut into pieces that will fit in the juicer.

CABBAGE

Benefits: Both red and green cabbage provide vitamin C, although the red variety has about twice as much as the green. Vitamin C is essential for building and repairing blood vessels, skin and connective tissues such as ligaments and tendons. It also aids in wound healing and keeps the immune system sharp. Red and green cabbage also provide a bit of iron, a mineral essential to healthy red blood cells, which carry oxygen to every cell in the body.

Preparation: Remove and discard loose, bruised or wilted leaves, then rinse the cabbage under cool running water. Cut the head in half, lay each half flat side down and cut into wedges.

CANTALOUPE

Benefits: If you want to arm your body with some of the best weapons for fighting heart disease, cancer, infections and more, cantaloupe is a sure bet. This sweet, juicy melon is rich in the cell-defending antioxidant beta-carotene, immunity-boosting vitamin C, and disease-fighting phytonutrients. It's also a good source of potassium, which helps the body get rid of excess sodium; excess sodium can contribute to high blood pressure and stroke risk in susceptible individuals.

Preparation: Hold the cantaloupe under cool running water and use a vegetable brush to scrub the netted surface clean. Cut the melon in half and scoop out the stringy seeds, then cut the halves into wedges and remove the rind.

CARROTS

Benefits: It's no myth: Carrots really are good for eyesight. The abundant vitamin A, in the form of beta-carotene, helps protect the eyes from vision stealers like night blindness, cataracts and macular degeneration. Vitamin A also helps to keep the body's outer shield—the skin—supple and strong.

Preparation: Wash carrots under cool running water, using a stiff-bristled vegetable brush to remove dirt and debris.

CAULIFLOWER

Benefits: You might think cauliflower's pale color means it's low in health-promoting constituents, but cauliflower comes in second only to citrus fruits in vitamin C content. Research suggests vitamin C may help defend blood vessels from damage and possibly slow the hardening of arteries that can lead to heart attack and stroke. Plus, the natural chemical that gives cauliflower its sharp taste may help fight cancers of the breast and prostate.

Preparation: Remove outer leaves, trim brown spots, break into florets and wash under cool running water.

CELERY

Benefits: Despite the fact that it is mostly water, celery supplies essential vitamins A, C and K as well as the minerals folic acid, which can help prevent certain birthbirth defects, and potassium, which helps regulate blood pressure. Celery also contains phytonutrients called phthalides, which recent research suggests may help protect the brain from oxidative stress and so may prove useful in keeping diseases such as Alzheimer's and Parkinson's at bay.

Preparation: Separate into stalks, trim the greens and any dried-out ends, and wash the stalks well under cool running water.

CHERRIES

Benefits: Both sweet and tart (sour) cherries provide disease-fighting antioxidants such as beta-carotene and vitamin C, which help defend the body's cells from damage. Both also offer potassium, the mineral that helps the body get rid of excess sodium. But tart cherries actually pack more nutrients. Recent research also suggests tart cherries can help fight inflammation, which can be beneficial in various ways, from easing arthritis pain and muscle soreness to potentially lowering the risk of heart disease.

Preparation: Remove the stems, then wash cherries thoroughly under cool running water and remove the pits.

CHILE PEPPERS

Benefits: Early research suggests capsaicin, the substance that gives chiles their characteristic bite, may help improve insulin's ability to lower blood sugar after meals. If these findings are confirmed, chile peppers could prove a useful tool in helping to prevent and treat type 2 diabetes. Chile peppers are also rich in beta-carotene and vitamin C, two antioxidants that can help prevent heart disease, cancer and other chronic diseases.

Preparation: Wash chile peppers well under cool running water. Wear gloves and avoid touching your eyes when handling chile peppers, and wash your hands, utensils and cutting board with soap and water afterwards. Cut off the stem end, slice the pepper down the center and feed pieces into the juicer. (For a less spicy juice, remove and discard the seeds and fiery white membrane.)

CILANTRO

Benefits: Fresh cilantro provides vitamin K, which is essential for proper blood clotting, as well as the minerals iron, magnesium and manganese. Iron is vital for healthy red blood cells, which transport oxygen to the body's cells; magnesium and manganese are important for proper metabolism. Fresh cilantro also contains phytonutrients that may help protect us against cancer.

Preparation: Discard any yellowed or wilted leaves and wash the cilantro under cool running water. Blot dry with a paper towel and either roll sprigs into a tight ball or place them between pieces of firmer produce and feed them into the juicer.

COCONUT WATER

Found inside young, green coconuts, coconut water is a clear liquid with a sweet, coconutty flavor. It should not be confused with white-colored coconut milk, which is pressed from the meat of mature coconuts. Unlike coconut meat and milk, coconut water is low in calories and fat free, so it's a healthier way to add coconut flavor to your juice. It is also rich in electrolytes, such as potassium, making it great for rehydration. Since immature coconuts are not readily available in most U.S. grocery stores, you'll need to purchase prepackaged coconut water to add to your juices.

CRANBERRIES

Benefits: Phytonutrients in cranberries prevent certain bacteria from sticking to the walls of the urinary tract, thus helping to prevent and treat urinary tract infections and interstitial cystitis (a condition causing bladder and pelvic discomfort). The same antibacterial action may also help to prevent gum disease and stomach ulcers, which are commonly caused by bacteria. Cranberries also offer phytonutrients that can help protect against disease of the heart and eyes.

Preparation: Wash cranberries thoroughly under cool running water, removing any shriveled or bruised berries.

CUCUMBERS

Benefits: Although cucumbers are mostly water, they do provide a decent dose of potassium, the essential mineral that's important for muscle contraction, nerve transmission, fluid balance and proper functioning of the heart and kidneys.

Preparation: Wash cucumbers thoroughly under cool running water. Tougher-skinned varieties should be peeled prior to juicing; softer-skinned cucumbers may simply need to be cut up to fit in the juicer.

CURRANTS

Benefits: Both black and red currants pack plenty of vitamin C, which helps keep the immune system functioning well. Red currants are also rich in antioxidants that help protect the body's cells from damage caused by unstable oxygen molecules, the kind of damage that can lead to heart disease, cancer and other health problems. Black currants are a good source of two essential minerals: manganese, which is important for bone structure, and potassium, which plays many roles, including helping to regulate body fluids and blood pressure.

Preparation: Wash currants thoroughly under cool running water.

FENNEL

Benefits: Low-calorie fennel offers vitamin C for a healthy immune system; calcium for strong bones; iron for plentiful red blood cells, which deliver life-sustaining oxygen to all the cells of the body; folate to help prevent neural tube birth defects; and potassium to balance out the sodium in our diets and keep blood pressure in check.

Preparation: Rinse fennel thoroughly under cool running water, making sure to remove dirt from the bulb and between the stalks. If necessary, cut the bulb into pieces that will fit in the juicer.

GARLIC

Benefits: Much of garlic's healing power appears to stem from allicin, the compound that makes the bulb so pungent when crushed, chopped or cooked. Studies suggest garlic can aid in lowering blood pressure and slowing the clogging of arteries that can lead to heart attack and stroke. It appears to have some anti-cancer effects, as well. Garlic also thins the blood (so if you consume a lot of it, alert your doctor before having any kind of surgery) and appears to have antibacterial and antiviral properties.

Preparation: Peel the desired number of cloves and feed them into the juicer with larger pieces of produce.

GINGER

Benefits: Research indicates that ginger is helpful for relieving the symptoms of motion sickness, morning sickness during pregnancy and nausea associated with chemotherapy. Indeed, ginger has been valued for its digestion-soothing effects for centuries. It's also filled with phytonutrients that act against inflammation, which may help explain its apparent ability to reduce joint pain, swelling and stiffness in people with arthritis. Ginger's anti-inflammatory actions may also prove beneficial for combatting cancer, heart disease and the growing list of other diseases that are being linked to chronic inflammation in the body.

Preparation: Use a sharp knife to peel off the tough skin that encases the entire root. If you purchase young ginger with very thin skin, no peeling is necessary.

GRAPEFRUIT

Benefits: Grapefruit is packed with vitamin C, and the pink and red varieties also offer plentiful vitamin A in the form of beta-carotene. These vitamins, along with another antioxidant phytonutrient called lycopene, help protect cells from the type of everyday damage that can lead to cancer and other chronic diseases. Grapefruit also contains phytonutrients that protect against certain types of eye disease.

Preparation: Wash under cool running water and remove the peel.

GRAPES

Benefits: Grapes, especially the red and purple varieties, contain powerful health-preserving phytonutrients that have shown promise in fighting cancer and lowering the risk of heart disease and stroke by reducing potentially damaging blood clots, improving blood flow and interfering with the process that deposits cholesterol on artery walls. Although much of the phytonutrient content is in the skins, the heat produced during the juicing process may help transfer some of that content to the juice.

Preparation: Wash grapes under cool running water and remove them from their stems.

GREENS

Benefits: Leafy greens—such as beet, turnip, collard, mustard and dandelion—have more antioxidants than many other fruits and vegetables, meaning they can help protect the cells in your body from damage. They also provide calcium, which is important for strong bones and teeth as well as proper muscle function and the transmission of impulses through the nerves.

Preparation: Wash greens well under cool running water and discard tough stems. Roll greens into a ball or place them between firm produce to feed them into the juicer.

HONEY

Honey appears to have some mild antibacterial and antioxidant properties; darker honeys may contain more of these. Some research also suggests that honey may help calm coughs and soothe irritated mucous membranes, such as those lining the throat.

HONEYDEW

Benefits: Honeydew melon is an excellent source of vitamin C, which is essential for the formation and repair of collagen, a type of tissue that holds the body's cells and tissues together and is a primary component of blood vessels. Vitamin C also promotes the normal development of bones and teeth. Honeydew provides some calcium, which helps keep bones and teeth strong, and iron, which is needed to transport oxygen to the body's cells.

Preparation: Wash the melon under cool running water, using a vegetable brush to scrub the rind. Cut the melon in half and scoop out the stringy seeds, then cut the halves into wedges and remove the rind.

JICAMA

Benefits: Low-calorie, low-sodium jicama is an excellent source of vitamin C, which helps fuel your immune system; promotes healthy bones, teeth and gums; and helps protect blood vessels from damage that can lead to heart attack or stroke.

Preparation: Wash jicama under cool running water, using a vegetable brush to clean the skin. Cut into large pieces, if necessary.

KALE

Benefits: Kale stands a head above other greens as an excellent source of beta-carotene and vitamin C, two antioxidants believed to be major players in the body's battle against cancer, heart disease and certain age-related declines in vision and cognitive function. Kale is packed with readily absorbed calcium, a mineral that is vital to warding off the bone-thinning disease osteoporosis and may also help keep blood pressure in a healthy range. Kale also provides decent amounts of folate, iron and potassium.

Preparation: Wash kale thoroughly under cool running water to remove dirt and sand from the leaves, and remove any tough center stems. Roll the leaves into a ball or slip them between firmer pieces of produce to feed them into the juicer.

KIWI

Benefits: One medium kiwi provides an entire day's worth of vitamin C, which not only helps maintain a strong immune system and healthy teeth and gums but may protect the arteries—including those feeding the heart and brain—from damage. Kiwi also packs potassium for healthy blood pressure and the antioxidants lutein and zeaxanthin, which safeguard eye health.

Preparation: Wash kiwi under cool running water and remove the peel. Cut into smaller pieces, if necessary.

LEMONS

Benefits: Lemons are loaded with vitamin C, a nutrient the body needs to heal wounds and perform all sorts of daily maintenance. For example, vitamin C is required for making collagen, a protein the body uses to grow and repair blood vessels, skin, cartilage, ligaments, tendons and bones. Vitamin C also helps ward off inflammation, heart disease and cancer.

Preparation: Wash lemons well under cool running water and remove the peel.

LIMES

Benefits: In addition to packing a powerful vitamin C punch, limes are full of an antioxidant phytochemical called limonin, which has shown anticancer, anti-inflammatory, antiviral and cholesterol-lowering effects in laboratory tests.

Preparation: Wash limes well under cool running water and remove the peel.

MANGOES

Benefits: Mangoes are a superior source of beta-carotene, a vitamin A precursor and antioxidant linked to a reduced risk of some forms of cancer. And a single mango offers nearly a full day's supply of vitamin C, a powerful antioxidant and important player in the body's ability to prevent infection. Mangoes also contribute calcium, potassium and magnesium, and regularly consuming foods rich in these minerals is associated with lower blood pressure.

Preparation: Wash mangoes thoroughly under cool running water before removing the peel and large pits.

MINT

Benefits: Mints, including the familiar peppermint and spearmint, offer vitamin C and beta-carotene, both of which have disease-fighting antioxidant actions. They also supply manganese, which is necessary for the body to properly metabolize carbohydrates and fats. In addition, a phytonutrient in mint appears to help block production of leukotrienes, molecules that trigger inflammation in the nasal passages, causing stuffiness. And the oil within the peppermint plant has a long history of helping to calm intestinal cramping and other discomforts of the digestive tract.

Preparation: Wash mint thoroughly by swishing it in a bowl of cold water, then blot it dry with a paper towel. Roll the sprigs into a ball or sandwich them between more substantial produce, and feed into the juicer.

ONIONS

Benefits: Onions provide some of the same heart- and brain-protecting effects as their cousin garlic does. They appear to help reduce blood clotting and lower damaging levels of cholesterol in the blood, which together can help prevent the narrowing and eventual blockage of arteries that can lead to heart attack and stroke. They also supply phytonutrients that fight inflammation, which many experts believe is a contributing factor in a host of chronic diseases, from cancer and heart disease to arthritis, asthma and type 2 diabetes. One such phytonutrient, quercetin, may help relieve chronic inflammation of the prostate and possibly even help fight allergies.

Preparation: Remove the papery skin, wash under cool running water and cut into pieces that will fit in the juicer.

ORANGES

Benefits: A single orange packs more than a day's worth of your vitamin C requirement. This antioxidant vitamin helps protect tissues and organs from damage; fuels immune function to protect us against infections; and plays a role in maintaining healthy blood vessels, bones, teeth and gums. The folate in oranges is important for women in their childbearing years as it helps prevent certain birth defects. And the potassium is beneficial for keeping blood pressure under control.

Preparation: Wash oranges well under cool running water and remove the peel.

PAPAYA

Benefits: Papayas pack plenty of potassium, a mineral that's essential for proper fluid balance, blood-pressure regulation and the health of your kidneys. As you might guess from their vibrant orange flesh, papayas are also loaded with the beta-carotene form of vitamin A as well as plenty of vitamin C, both of which help fight cancer and heart disease.

Preparation: Wash the papaya well under cool running water. Cut it in half lengthwise and use a spoon to scoop out the seeds. Then cut it into pieces that will fit in the juicer.

PARSLEY

Benefits: Parsley is good for more than freshening your breath with its chlorophyll. Early research suggests it may have some benefit in lowering blood sugar, which is promising news for people with diabetes. Parsley also contains powerful phytonutrients called flavonoids, along with beta-carotene and vitamin C, which may help protect blood vessels from inflammation and damage that can lead to vision loss, heart attack and stroke.

Preparation: Wash parsley thoroughly by swishing it in a bowl of cold water, then blot it dry with a paper towel. Roll the sprigs into a ball or sandwich them between more substantial produce, and feed into the juicer.

PARSNIPS

Benefits: Parsnips are a good source of folate, an essential B vitamin the body needs to form oxygen-carrying red blood cells. Folate also appears to help lower the risk of heart disease and can help women of childbearing age prevent certain birth defects in their offspring. Parsnips supply ample amounts of potassium, which is needed to regulate blood pressure.

Preparation: Wash parsnips under cool running water, using a stiff-bristled vegetable brush to remove dirt and debris.

PEACHES

Benefits: Peaches are a sweet and low-calorie source of nutrients that can help protect the body from damage that can lead to chronic disease. But peaches and other produce that contain similar nutrients may be especially beneficial for people with diabetes, because the beta-carotene and vitamin C in the fruit may help prevent or delay some of the complications of diabetes, such as nerve damage and vision loss. Peaches are also a rich source of potassium, an essential mineral that can help keep blood pressure in a healthy range.

Preparation: Wash peaches gently in cool running water. Cut the fruit in half and remove the pits.

PEARS

Benefits: Pears provide vitamin C and the mineral copper, which work as antioxidants in the body to help protect cells, tissues and organs from damage caused by unstable molecules called free radicals. Pears also supply both calcium and boron, essential minerals important to bone health. Calcium is required for building and maintaining bone, and boron helps the body use the calcium it takes in.

Preparation: Remove the stems, wash the pears thoroughly under cool running water and, if necessary, cut them in half to fit in the juicer.

PINEAPPLE

Benefits: Pineapples are virtually dripping with vitamin C, the antioxidant that's also essential for keeping your immune system revved up to resist colds, flu and other infections. On top of that, a cup of pineapple supplies more than the recommended daily intake of manganese, an essential mineral that plays a role in energy production and helps keep bones strong. This tropical treat also offers decent amounts of copper, for proper brain and nerve function, and folate, which can help prevent certain birth defects. Fresh, raw pineapple contains the enzyme bromelain, a digestive aid that helps prevent inflammation and swelling, too.

Preparation: Wash the pineapple and use a vegetable brush to scrub the skin. Cut a small slice from the bottom and cut off the top of the fruit. Stand the pineapple on a cutting board and use a sharp knife to cut away the skin. Remove any remaining eyes with the tip of a knife or vegetable peeler and cut the whole peeled pineapple into quarters.

PLUMS

Benefits: Plums provide vitamins A and C as well as potassium. The vitamins are cell defenders that can help keep chronic disease at bay, while potassium is important for fluid balance, blood pressure regulation and a steady heartbeat.

Preparation: Wash plums gently but thoroughly in cool running water. Cut the fruit in half and remove the pits.

POMEGRANATES

Benefits: Pomegranates are truly a heart's delight. They supply a rich dose of potassium for maintaining a steady heartbeat and healthy blood pressure. Their juice is full of heart-protective antioxidants, with nearly three times the antioxidant content of red wine or green tea. Pomegranate juice may also help reduce the buildup and lower blood levels of artery-clogging cholesterol and improve blood flow.

Preparation: Wash pomegranates well under cool running water, then cut into pieces. (The juice can stain, so consider wearing gloves and an apron.) Immerse the pieces in a bowl of cold water to pry off the seeds. The membrane that holds the seeds in place will float to the top; it has a bitter taste, so discard it. Collect the seeds and feed them into the juicer. For convenience, you can find containers of ready-to-use pomegranate seeds in the refrigerated produce section of some supermarkets.

RADISHES

Benefits: Radishes offer calcium for strong bones and teeth; potassium for a steady heartbeat and lower blood pressure; iron for plenty of oxygen-carrying red blood cells; selenium for healthy hair, nails and muscles; and magnesium for proper nerve, muscle and immune function.

Preparation: Wash radishes under cool running water, using a vegetable brush to scrub away stuck-on dirt, if necessary.

RASPBERRIES

Benefits: Raspberries are an amazingly compact and delicious source of a slew of beneficial nutrients, including free radical-fighting vitamins A, C and E; essential minerals, including copper, iron, magnesium, manganese and potassium; and health-promoting phytochemicals, including phenolic compounds that have shown promise in battling cancer, inflammation (which may be behind a variety of chronic diseases, including heart disease) and degenerative nerve diseases, such as Alzheimer's.

Preparation: Wash berries gently but thoroughly under cool running water.

SPINACH

Benefits: Spinach has an incredibly rich and potent mix of essential nutrients with antioxidant functions, including vitamins A, C and E and the minerals manganese, selenium and zinc. Spinach also provides more than a dozen antioxidant and anti-inflammatory phytonutrients, making it helpful in fighting high blood pressure; hardening of the arteries and stroke; various cancers; and age-related eye diseases such as cataracts and macular degeneration. Spinach also contributes iron and folic acid for healthy oxygen-carrying red blood cells.

Preparation: Wash spinach leaves well under cool running water and discard tough stems. Roll the leaves into a ball or place them between firm produce to feed them into the juicer.

SPROUTS

Benefits: Sprouts are concentrated sources of several essential nutrients, including the antioxidant vitamin C and vitamin K, which plays an important role in proper blood clotting. Sprouts also contribute iron, for healthy red blood cells, and folate, which can help prevent certain birth defects when consumed in sufficient amount by women in their childbearing years.

Preparation: Place the sprouts in a colander under cool running water for at least two minutes, using your fingers to toss them like a salad so that they are thoroughly rinsed. Lay them on paper towels, cover with more paper towels and blot them dry. Wad up the sprouts or place them between pieces of other produce to feed them into the juicer.

STRAWBERRIES

Benefits: Strawberries contain a phytonutrient called ellagic acid that helps fight inflammation and cancer-causing cell damage. They're also a top source of immunity-boosting vitamin C, containing more of this antioxidant than oranges. Strawberries also supply lots of potassium, which helps the body regulate blood pressure and so may help prevent stroke.

Preparation: Wash berries well under cool running water and remove the green tops.

SWEET POTATOES

Benefits: Sweet potatoes provide a jaw-dropping amount of vitamin A in the form of antioxidant beta-carotene, making them an incredibly valuable tool in warding off chronic diseases such as cancer and heart disease, as well as diseases such as asthma and rheumatoid arthritis that involve inflammation. Sweet potatoes also pack a powerful vitamin C punch and a hefty load of potassium.

Preparation: Wash sweet potatoes under cool running water, using a vegetable brush to remove dirt and debris. If necessary, cut them into pieces that will fit in the juicer.

SWISS CHARD

Benefits: Swiss chard is loaded with antioxidant nutrients, including vitamins A and C, which help protect the body's cells from inflammation and damage caused by exposure to unstable oxygen molecules within the body and toxic substances from the environment. Swiss chard also contains phytonutrients that may help control blood sugar in people with type 2 diabetes.

Preparation: Wash Swiss chard under cool running water. Stack the leaves, roll them into a ball or bundle and feed them into the juicer.

TANGERINES

Benefits: Sweet, low-calorie tangerines are loaded with vitamin A in the form of beta-carotene, which can help prevent night blindness and protect the cells in the eyes and the rest of the body from damage caused by ultraviolet light, radiation, air pollution, cigarette smoke and other toxic substances. Tangerines also supply calcium, a mineral essential to strong bones and teeth and a steady heart rate.

Preparation: Wash tangerines under cool running water and remove the peel.

TOMATOES

Benefits: Research suggests that lycopene, the phytonutrient that gives tomatoes their red hue, may help reduce the risk of heart and blood vessel disease as well as prostate cancer. The carotenoids, including beta-carotene, are also powerful weapons against cardiovascular disease, cancer and other chronic ailments. Tomatoes also provide vitamin C for a strong immune system and potassium for healthy blood pressure.

Preparation: Wash tomatoes well under cool running water and remove any stems. If necessary, cut into halves or quarters.

TURNIPS

Benefits: Turnips contain lysine, an amino acid that's useful in preventing and treating cold sores. They also have some vitamin C, which the immune system needs to fight viruses, bacteria and other infectious agents. And turnips supply the minerals potassium and calcium, which work to keep blood pressure in a healthy range.

Preparation: Wash turnips well under cool running water; use a vegetable brush to remove stubborn dirt. Small turnips can go in the juicer unpeeled; larger turnips should be peeled and, if necessary, cut into smaller pieces before being fed into the juicer.

WATERCRESS

Benefits: Like its cruciferous cousins, including broccoli, cabbage and kale, watercress is rich in antioxidants, including beta-carotene and lutein, which help protect the eyes from damage and combat the deleterious effects of free radicals that can lead to the development and growth of cancer cells. Watercress has also been found to contain phytonutrients that aid detoxification and help protect the lungs from cancerous changes. Watercress also offers calcium and potassium, which are essential for a healthy heart.

Preparation: Rinse the leaves thoroughly under cool running water and pat them dry with a paper towel. Roll them into a ball or slip them between firm pieces of produce and feed them into the juicer.

WATERMELON

Benefits: Unlike other melons, watermelon is a valuable source of lycopene, the phytonutrient responsible for tomatoes' red hue. Research has shown that lycopene can reduce the risk of cancers of the breast, colon and prostate. Watermelon also provides disease-fighting antioxidants vitamin C and beta-carotene. And it offers a decent dose of potassium, which helps keep blood pressure in a healthy range and may reduce the risk of kidney stones and perhaps even bone loss.

Preparation: Wash the watermelon thoroughly under cool running water, then use a sharp knife to cut it into smaller pieces and remove the rind.

ZUCCHINI

Benefits: Zucchini provides the mineral folate along with vitamins A and C, all of which help to protect the cells in the heart and other parts of the body from damage that can lead to disease. Zucchini's potassium adds to the cardiovascular benefit of the vegetable by helping the body maintain a steady heartbeat and healthy blood pressure.

Preparation: Wash zucchini well under cool running water and, if the peel is waxy, remove the peel. (Removing the peel will also produce a milder-tasting juice.)

ALL THE EXTRAS

Boost the flavor and nutritional value of your juices and smoothies with a variety of healthful additions, including spices, seeds, powders and more.

AÇAÍ BERRIES: Most commonly found frozen, this Brazilian superfood is packed with antioxidants and fiber; it may help reduce cholesterol and blood pressure.

APPLE CIDER VINEGAR: With valuable probiotic and anti-inflammatory properties, this vinegar can aid in digestion and help the body maintain a healthy alkaline level. (Choose raw apple cider vinegar rather than the more widely available pasteurized version.)

BEE POLLEN: Contains all the essential amino acids (making it a complete protein) along with vitamins and minerals.

CHIA SEEDS: Packed with fiber, protein and omega-3 fatty acids, these seeds can dramatically increase the nutritional profile of your beverages while adding a slightly nutty flavor.

COCONUT MILK: Provides a big protein boost to smoothies while adding a mildly sweet, nutty coconut flavor. Pairs well with tropical fruits such as pineapple and mango.

COCONUT OIL: This superfood is anti-viral, anti-fungal, full of antioxidants and can help balance blood sugar and boost metabolism.

FLAXSEED OR FLAXSEED OIL: A good source of protein, fiber, omega-3 fatty acids and vitamin E, flaxseed can help lower cholesterol and reduce the risk of heart disease. Purchase ground flaxseed (rather than whole) for use in beverages.

GREEN TEA POWDER (MATCHA): High in antioxidants, vitamins, minerals and amino acids, matcha may help boost metabolism and lower blood sugar.

GROUND RED PEPPER OR JALAPEÑOS: An anti-inflammatory containing capsaicin, this spicy addition to your drinks may boost your immune system and fire up your metabolism.

HEMP SEEDS: An easily digestible complete protein that's also rich in omega-3 fatty acids, iron and magnesium, hemp seeds can be blended into any smoothie or juice without altering the flavor. (Look for shelled seeds called "hemp hearts" or hemp protein powder.)

NUT AND SEED BUTTERS: Add almond butter, peanut butter, sunflower seed butter or tahini to your smoothies for a delicious protein boost. The healthy fats and fiber in these butters help keep you feeling fuller for longer.

SPIRULINA: Made from an aquatic plant and packed with nutrients including vitamins, minerals, omega-3 fatty acids and protein, spirulina promotes dental health and may help lower bad cholesterol while increasing good cholesterol. It's best added to green smoothies along with some sweet fruit, as many find the flavor to be somewhat unpleasant.

TOFU: Blends beautifully into smoothies, adding high-quality complete protein and a creamy texture. It also pairs well with almost any ingredient.

TURMERIC: Promotes healthy metabolism and is also known for anti-inflammatory properties. This root vegetable can be grated into your drinks (or add ground turmeric instead); the flavor goes well with green smoothies and juice blends containing pineapple or carrots.

YOGURT (PREFERABLY GREEK OR ICELANDIC): Adds a significant amount of protein and a creamy texture to your smoothies.

Orange Fennel Sprout
(page 102)

APPLE

TANGY TWIST

makes 3 servings

1 grapefruit, peeled

4 carrots

1 apple

1 beet

1 inch fresh ginger, peeled

Ice cubes

Juice grapefruit, carrots, apple, beet and ginger. Stir. Serve over ice.

APPLE MELON JUICE >

makes 3 servings

¼ **honeydew melon, rind removed**
¼ **cantaloupe, rind removed**
1 **apple**
3 **leaves kale**
3 **leaves Swiss chard**
   Cantaloupe balls (optional)

Juice honeydew, cantaloupe, apple, kale and chard. Stir. Garnish with cantaloupe balls.

RAINBOW JUICE

makes 3 servings

8 **leaves Swiss chard**
1 **Asian pear**
1 **apple**
1 **beet**
1 **carrot**
¼ **head green cabbage**

Juice chard, pear, apple, beet, carrot and cabbage. Stir.

APPLE CARROT ZINGER >

makes 2 servings

4 carrots
2 apples
¼ cucumber
1 inch fresh ginger, peeled

Juice carrots, apples, cucumber and ginger. Stir.

ICED ORCHARD BLEND

makes 2 servings

3 plums
1 sweet apple
Ice cubes

Juice plums and apple. Stir. Serve over ice.

APPLE, TATER & CARROT >

makes 4 servings

4 apples
1 sweet potato
1 carrot

Juice apples, sweet potato and carrot. Stir.

TART APPLE GRAPE

makes 2 servings

3 green apples
1 cup green seedless grapes
¼ lemon, peeled

Juice apples, grapes and lemon. Stir.

CABBAGE PATCH JUICE >

makes 3 servings

2 **apples**
¼ **napa cabbage**
¼ **red cabbage**

Juice apples, napa cabbage and red cabbage. Stir.

KIWI APPLE PEAR

makes 2 servings

3 **kiwis, peeled**
2 **apples**
1 **pear**

Juice kiwis, apples and pear. Stir.

PARSNIP PARTY >

makes 2 servings

3 parsnips
1 apple
1 pear
½ bulb fennel
½ cup fresh parsley

Juice parsnips, apple, pear, fennel and parsley. Stir.

VEGGIE VOLCANO

makes 2 servings

2 carrots
1 cucumber
1 cup fresh spinach
½ apple
½ lemon, peeled
1 inch fresh ginger, peeled
¼ teaspoon ground cinnamon
⅛ teaspoon ground red pepper

Juice carrots, cucumber, spinach, apple, lemon and ginger. Stir in cinnamon and red pepper until well blended.

CUCUMBER APPLE ZINGER >

makes 2 servings

2 apples

½ **cucumber**

½ **inch fresh ginger, peeled**

Juice apples, cucumber and ginger. Stir.

FANTASTIC FIVE JUICE

makes 2 servings

1 tangerine, peeled

½ **peach**

½ **apple**

½ **pear**

½ **cup green seedless grapes**

Juice tangerine, peach, apple, pear and grapes. Stir.

FENNEL CABBAGE JUICE >

makes 2 servings

1 **apple**
¼ **small green cabbage**
½ **bulb fennel**
1 **lemon, peeled**
Fennel fronds (optional)

Juice apple, cabbage, fennel and lemon. Stir. Garnish with fennel fronds.

CRIMSON CARROT

makes 2 servings

½ **red cabbage**
2 **apples**
1 **carrot**
⅓ **cup red seedless grapes**
Ice cubes

Juice cabbage, apples, carrot and grapes. Stir. Serve over ice.

SUPER BETA-CAROTENE >

makes 2 servings

4 carrots

1 apple

4 leaves bok choy

2 leaves kale

½ inch fresh ginger, peeled

Carrot slices (optional)

Juice carrots, apple, bok choy, kale and ginger. Stir. Garnish with carrot slices.

CALCIUM-RICH JUICE

makes 2 servings

3 carrots

8 leaves collard greens

1 apple

1 red bell pepper

1 cup fresh cilantro

Juice carrots, collard greens, apple, bell pepper and cilantro. Stir.

KALE MELON >

makes 3 servings

4 **leaves kale**

2 **apples**

⅛ **seedless watermelon, rind removed**

½ **lemon, peeled**

Juice kale, apples, watermelon and lemon. Stir.

GRAPEFRUIT REFRESHER

makes 2 servings

1 **grapefruit, peeled**

1 **apple**

½ **cucumber**

¼ **beet**

2 **leaves Swiss chard**

Juice grapefruit, apple, cucumber, beet and chard. Stir.

HEADACHE BUSTER >

makes 1 serving

1 cup cauliflower florets
1 cup broccoli florets
1 apple

Juice cauliflower, broccoli and apple. Stir.

CITRUS BLUSH

makes 2 servings

1 grapefruit, peeled
1 peach
1 apple

Juice grapefruit, peach and apple. Stir.

AUTUMN APPLE PIE JUICE >

makes 2 servings

2 apples

½ butternut squash, peeled

¼ teaspoon pumpkin pie spice,
   plus additional for garnish

   Cinnamon sticks (optional)

Juice apples and squash. Stir in ¼ teaspoon pumpkin pie spice until well blended. Garnish with additional pumpkin pie spice and cinnamon sticks.

GARDEN JUICE

makes 2 servings

2 carrots

1 yellow bell pepper

1 apple

1 cup broccoli florets

1 beet

½ sweet potato

1 cup fresh parsley

Juice carrots, bell pepper, apple, broccoli, beet, sweet potato and parsley. Stir.

TONGUE TWISTER >

makes 2 servings

2 **apples**
1½ **cups arugula**
½ **cup fresh cilantro**
½ **jalapeño pepper**
1 **cup coconut water**

Juice apples, arugula, cilantro and jalapeño pepper. Stir in coconut water until well blended.

POTATO APPLE

makes 1 serving

2 **potatoes**
2 **sweet apples**

Juice potatoes and apples. Stir.

RUBY APPLE STINGER >

makes 2 servings

2 beets

2 carrots

½ apple

1 inch fresh ginger, peeled

¼ lemon, peeled

Juice beets, carrots, apple, ginger and lemon. Stir.

DRINKABLE SLAW

makes 2 servings

2 cups broccoli florets

½ small red cabbage

2 carrots

1 apple

½ lemon, peeled

½ inch fresh ginger, peeled

Juice broccoli, cabbage, carrots, apple, lemon and ginger. Stir.

TRIPLE PEPPER >

makes 2 servings

2 apples
1 red bell pepper
1 yellow bell pepper
½ jalapeño pepper

Juice apples, bell peppers and jalapeño pepper. Stir.

APRICOT APPLE

makes 1 serving

4 apricots
2 red apples

Juice apricots and apples. Stir.

WORKOUT WARMUP >

makes 2 servings

2 apples
2 kiwis, peeled
4 leaves kale
½ lime, peeled

Juice apples, kiwis, kale and lime. Stir.

PEAR-CARROT-APPLE JUICE

makes 2 servings

2 pears
2 carrots
1 apple

Juice pears, carrots and apple. Stir.

POMEGRANATE APPLE >

makes 2 servings

2 pomegranates, peeled

2 apples

Juice pomegranate seeds and apples. Stir.

REALLY RHUBARB

makes 2 servings

3 apples

2 stalks rhubarb

Juice apples and rhubarb. Stir.

WHEATGRASS BLAST >

makes 2 servings

2 **apples**

2 **cups wheatgrass**

1 **lemon, peeled**

6 **sprigs fresh mint**

Lemon peel twists (optional)

Juice apples, wheatgrass, lemon and mint. Stir. Garnish with lemon twists.

SPICED APPLE

makes 1 serving

2 **apples**

1 **lime, peeled**

Pinch ground cinnamon

Juice apples and lime. Stir in cinnamon.

SHARP APPLE COOLER >

makes 3 servings

3 **apples**
1 **cucumber**
¼ **cup fresh mint**
1 **inch fresh ginger, peeled**

Juice apples, cucumber, mint and ginger. Stir.

KIWI FIZZ

makes 2 servings

2 **red apples**
3 **kiwis, peeled**
  Sparkling water

Juice apples and kiwis. Stir. Top with sparkling water.

MELONADE >

makes 4 servings

¼ **seedless watermelon, rind removed**

1 **apple**

1 **lemon, peeled**

Juice watermelon, apple and lemon. Stir.

CAROTENE WITH A KICK

makes 2 servings

2 **carrots**

1 **apple**

1 **cup radicchio**

4 **leaves Swiss chard**

2 **radishes**

½ **lime, peeled**

Juice carrots, apple, radicchio, chard, radishes and lime. Stir.

COOL APPLE MANGO >

makes 2 servings

1 mango, peeled
1 apple
1 cucumber
½ inch fresh ginger, peeled
Mango wedges (optional)

Juice mango, apple, cucumber and ginger. Stir. Garnish with mango wedges.

SIMPLE GARDEN BLEND

makes 2 servings

3 carrots
2 apples
1 zucchini

Juice carrots, apples and zucchini. Stir.

CUCUMBER BASIL COOLER >

makes 2 servings

1 cucumber

1 apple

½ cup fresh basil

½ lime, peeled

Sprigs fresh basil (optional)

Juice cucumber, apple, basil and lime. Stir. Garnish with basil sprigs.

GREAT GRAPE JUICE

makes 1 serving

1 cup red seedless grapes

1 red apple

¼ cup cherries, pitted

½ lemon, peeled

Juice grapes, apple, cherries and lemon. Stir.

CARROT-BEET-APPLE

makes 2 servings

3 carrots
2 beets
2 apples

Juice carrots, beets and apples. Stir.

APPLE BROCCOLI

makes 1 serving

2 apples
¾ cup broccoli florets

Juice apple and broccoli. Stir.

PEAR CABBAGE JUICE

makes 2 servings

¼ **red cabbage**

1 **Asian pear**

1 **apple**

1 **carrot**

½ **lime, peeled**

½ **inch fresh ginger, peeled**

Juice cabbage, pear, apple, carrot, lime and ginger. Stir.

SPROUT-APPLE-CARROT

makes 2 servings

2 **apples**

1 **carrot**

1 **cup alfalfa sprouts**

1 **cup bean sprouts**

4 **sprigs fresh parsley**

Juice apples, carrot, alfalfa sprouts, bean sprouts and parsley. Stir.

BERRY

PURPLEBERRY JUICE

makes 2 servings

2 **cups red seedless grapes**

1 **apple**

½ **cup blackberries**

½ **inch fresh ginger, peeled**

Juice grapes, apple, blackberries and ginger. Stir.

JICAMA FRUIT COMBO >

makes 2 servings

1½ **cups strawberries**

1 **cup cut-up peeled jicama**

1 **apple**

½ **cucumber**

2 **sprigs fresh mint (optional)**

Juice strawberries, jicama, apple and cucumber. Stir. Garnish with mint.

MONKEYING AROUND

makes 2 servings

1 **banana**

2 **tart apples**

2 **cups blackberries**

1 **lemon, peeled**

Juice banana, apples, blackberries and lemon. Stir.

ORCHARD CRUSH >

makes 2 servings

2 apples
1 cup raspberries
1 cup strawberries

Juice apples, raspberries and strawberries. Stir.

GREEN BERRY BOOSTER

makes 2 servings

1 cup blueberries
1 cucumber
1 apple
4 leaves collard greens, Swiss chard or kale
½ lemon, peeled

Juice blueberries, cucumber, apple, collard greens and lemon. Stir.

CRANBERRY APPLE TWIST >

makes 3 servings

2 **apples**

¾ **cup cranberries**

½ **cucumber**

½ **lemon, peeled**

1 **inch fresh ginger, peeled**

Juice apples, cranberries, cucumber, lemon and ginger. Stir.

BERRY GOOD JUICE

makes 1 serving

2 **apples**

¾ **cup blueberries**

¾ **cup blackcurrants or blueberries**

1 **teaspoon honey**

Juice apples, blueberries and blackcurrants. Stir in honey until well blended.

PEAR RASPBERRY >

2 **pears**

2 **cups raspberries, plus**
   additional for garnish

½ **cucumber**

Pear slices (optional)

Juice pears, 2 cups raspberries and cucumber. Stir. Garnish with pear slices and additional raspberries.

RUBY JEWEL

2 **cups strawberries**

1½ **cups cranberries**

1 **orange, peeled**

Ice cubes

Juice strawberries, cranberries and orange. Stir. Serve over ice.

SUNSET BERRY >

makes 2 servings

1 cup strawberries

1 orange, peeled

½ lime, peeled

Lime slices (optional)

Juice strawberries, orange and lime. Stir. Garnish with lime slices.

WATERMELON RASPBERRY

makes 3 servings

¼ seedless watermelon, rind removed

1 cup raspberries

Ice cubes

Juice watermelon and raspberries. Stir. Serve over ice.

SWEET & SOUR >

makes 2 servings

1½ **cups raspberries**
⅛ **papaya**
½ **grapefruit, peeled**

Juice raspberries, papaya and grapefruit. Stir.

MINTY BERRY-ADE

makes 1 serving

1 **to 2 handfuls fresh spinach**
1 **cup strawberries**
½ **cucumber**
1 **lemon, peeled**
2 **to 3 sprigs fresh mint**

Juice spinach, strawberries, cucumber, lemon and mint. Stir.

CRANBERRY PEAR BLAST >

makes 2 servings

2 **pears**

½ **cucumber**

¾ **cup fresh or thawed frozen cranberries**

¼ **lemon, peeled**

½ **to 1 inch fresh ginger, peeled**

Juice pears, cucumber, cranberries, lemon and ginger. Stir.

CURRANT EVENT

makes 2 servings

1½ **cups strawberries**

1¼ **cups red currants**

1 **orange, peeled**

1 **teaspoon honey (optional)**

Juice strawberries, currants and orange. Stir in honey, if desired, until well blended.

REFRESHING STRAWBERRY JUICE >

makes 2 servings

2 cups strawberries

1 cucumber

¼ lemon, peeled

Juice strawberries, cucumber and lemon. Stir.

BLUE BANANA JUICE

makes 1 serving

1 ripe banana

2 cups blueberries

Juice banana and blueberries. Stir.

PRETTY IN PINK >

makes 3 servings

¼ **seedless watermelon, rind removed**

1½ **cups cranberries**

½ **cucumber**

Juice watermelon, cranberries and cucumber. Stir.

CRANBERRY COCONUT

makes 1 serving

2 **cups fresh spinach**

½ **cup cranberries**

½ **cucumber**

2 **sprigs fresh mint**

¼ **cup coconut water**

Juice spinach, cranberries, cucumber and mint. Stir in coconut water until well blended.

MELON RASPBERRY MEDLEY >

makes 2 servings

⅛ **honeydew melon, rind removed**

⅛ **seedless watermelon, rind removed**

⅓ **cup raspberries**

Ice cubes

Juice honeydew, watermelon and raspberries. Stir. Serve over ice.

WELLNESS JUICE

makes 2 servings

2 **apples**

¼ **small red cabbage**

2 **zucchini**

1 **orange, peeled**

1 **cup blueberries**

6 **leaves kale**

½ **cucumber**

Juice apples, cabbage, zucchini, orange, blueberries, kale and cucumber. Stir.

SUPER BERRY REFRESHER >

makes 2 servings

1 **cup strawberries**

1 **cup raspberries**

1 **cucumber**

½ **cup blackberries**

½ **cup blueberries**

¼ **lemon, peeled**

Juice strawberries, raspberries, cucumber, blackberries, blueberries and lemon. Stir.

MELON BERRY GREEN JUICE

makes 2 servings

¼ **small watermelon, rind removed**

1 **pear**

1 **cup blueberries**

4 **leaves collard greens**

1 **lime, peeled**

Juice watermelon, pear, blueberries, collard greens and lime. Stir.

BLUEBERRY HAZE >

makes 2 servings

2 **apples**

1½ **cups blueberries**

½ **grapefruit, peeled**

1 **inch fresh ginger, peeled**

Juice apples, blueberries, grapefruit and ginger. Stir.

STRAWBERRY MELON

makes 2 servings

½ **cantaloupe, rind removed**

1 **cup strawberries**

Juice cantaloupe and strawberries. Stir.

BANANA BLACKBERRY

makes 1 serving

1 **ripe banana**

1 **cup blackberries**

½ **lemon, peeled**

Juice banana, blackberries and lemon. Stir.

FRUITY VEGETABLE JUICE

makes 1 serving

1 **carrot**

1 **cup fresh spinach**

½ **cup blueberries**

¼ **beet**

Juice carrot, spinach, blueberries and beet. Stir.

APPLEBERRY JUICE

makes 2 servings

2 **apples**
1½ **cups strawberries**
¼ **lemon, peeled**

Juice apples, strawberries and lemon. Stir.

BLUEBERRY GRAPE

makes 1 serving

1 **handful red seedless grapes**
1 **cup blueberries, fresh or thawed frozen**

Juice grapes and blueberries. Stir.

CELERY

UP AND AT 'EM

makes 1 serving

2 cups fresh spinach

1 apple

1 carrot

1 stalk celery

¼ lemon, peeled

1 inch fresh ginger, peeled

Apple and orange slices (optional)

Juice spinach, apple, carrot, celery, lemon and ginger. Stir. Garnish with apple and orange slices.

ORANGE FENNEL SPROUT >

makes 2 servings

2 oranges, peeled

2 stalks celery

1 bulb fennel

1 cup alfalfa sprouts

Juice oranges, celery, fennel and alfalfa sprouts. Stir.

VEGGIE BLAST

makes 2 servings

3 stalks celery

1 beet

1 carrot

1 red bell pepper

1 apple

6 leaves kale

½ cup fresh cilantro

1 inch fresh ginger, peeled

½ teaspoon ground turmeric

Juice celery, beet, carrot, bell pepper, apple, kale, cilantro and ginger. Stir in turmeric until well blended.

SPICY APPLE PEACH >

> makes 3 servings

2 apples

6 leaves mustard greens

2 stalks celery, plus additional for garnish

1 kiwi, peeled

1 peach

Juice apples, mustard greens, 2 stalks celery, kiwi and peach. Stir. Garnish with additional celery.

CHERRY GREEN

> makes 2 servings

1 cup cherries, pitted

2 stalks celery

1 apple

1 cup fresh parsley

1 lemon, peeled

Juice cherries, celery, apple, parsley and lemon. Stir.

SWEET & GREEN >

makes 2 servings

1 cup broccoli florets
¼ pineapple, peeled
2 stalks celery

Juice broccoli, pineapple and celery. Stir.

ZIPPY PINEAPPLE CELERY

makes 2 servings

½ pineapple, peeled
2 radishes
1 stalk celery

Juice pineapple, radishes and celery. Stir.

AMAZING GREEN JUICE >

makes 2 servings

1 cucumber

1 green apple

2 stalks celery, plus
   additional for garnish

½ bulb fennel

3 leaves kale

Juice cucumber, apple, 2 stalks celery, fennel and kale. Stir. Garnish with additional celery.

GAZPACHO IN A GLASS

makes 4 servings

3 tomatoes

2 cucumbers

3 stalks celery

1 apple

1 lemon, peeled

1 green onion

¼ cup fresh cilantro

1 chile pepper

1 clove garlic

Pinch black pepper

Juice tomatoes, cucumbers, celery, apple, lemon, green onion, cilantro, chile pepper and garlic. Stir in black pepper until well blended.

GREEN QUEEN >

makes 2 servings

1 cup fresh spinach

2 stalks celery

5 leaves kale

1 cup fresh cilantro

½ cucumber

½ apple

½ lemon, peeled

½ inch fresh ginger, peeled

Sprigs fresh cilantro (optional)

Juice spinach, celery, kale, cilantro, cucumber, apple, lemon and ginger. Stir. Garnish with cilantro sprigs.

SPICY CELERY

makes 2 servings

3 stalks celery

2 pears

½ bulb fennel

½ cucumber

2 fresh sage leaves

1 sprig fresh oregano

Worcestershire sauce or tamari soy sauce

Juice celery, pears, fennel, cucumber, sage and oregano. Stir in Worcestershire sauce to taste.

KALE-APPLE-CARROT >

makes 2 servings

3 carrots

2 stalks celery

1 apple

3 leaves kale

½ cup fresh parsley

Juice carrots, celery, apple, kale and parsley. Stir.

HEART HEALTHY JUICE

makes 2 servings

2 tomatoes

1 cup broccoli florets

1 cucumber

1 stalk celery

1 carrot

½ lemon, peeled

1 clove garlic

Juice tomatoes, broccoli, cucumber, celery, carrot, lemon and garlic. Stir.

MINT JULEP JUICE >

makes 1 serving

1 **apple**
1 **cup fresh spinach**
1 **stalk celery**
1 **cup fresh mint**
  Apple wedge (optional)

Juice apple, spinach, celery and mint. Stir. Garnish with apple wedge.

BITE-YOU-BACK VEGGIE JUICE

makes 2 servings

3 **carrots**
1 **cucumber**
1 **apple**
2 **stalks celery**
3 **leaves mustard greens**

Juice carrots, cucumber, apple, celery and mustard greens. Stir.

APPLE-K JUICE >

makes 2 servings

1 kiwi, peeled

1 apple

4 leaves kale

1 stalk celery

½ lemon, peeled

Kiwi slices (optional)

Juice kiwi, apple, kale, celery and lemon. Stir. Garnish with kiwi slices.

HIGH-C COCKTAIL

makes 2 servings

¼ small green cabbage

3 carrots

4 stalks celery

Juice cabbage, carrots and celery. Stir.

VEGGIE DELIGHT >

makes 2 servings

1 carrot
1 stalk celery
1 beet
1 apple
½ small sweet onion

Juice carrot, celery, beet, apple and onion. Stir.

YELLOWBELLY

makes 2 servings

¼ cantaloupe, rind removed
1 pear
2 parsnips
¾ cup cut-up peeled celery root
½ inch fresh ginger, peeled

Juice cantaloupe, pear, parsnips, celery root and ginger. Stir.

BEDTIME COCKTAIL >

makes 2 servings

½ **head romaine lettuce**

2 **stalks celery, plus additional for garnish**

½ **cucumber**

Juice romaine, 2 stalks celery and cucumber. Stir. Garnish with additional celery.

CUCUMBER CELERY JUICE

makes 1 serving

½ **cucumber**

1 **stalk celery**

Juice cucumber and celery. Stir.

SWEET CELERY >

makes 2 servings

3 stalks celery
1 apple
1 lemon, peeled
¼ cup raspberries

Juice celery, apple, lemon and raspberries. Stir.

MIGRAINE BLASTER

makes 2 servings

3 carrots
3 apples
1 cup red seedless grapes
1 tomato
1 stalk celery

Juice carrots, apples, grapes, tomato and celery. Stir.

CLEANSING GREEN JUICE >

makes 2 servings

4 leaves bok choy

1 stalk celery

½ cucumber

¼ bulb fennel

½ lemon, peeled

Juice bok choy, celery, cucumber, fennel and lemon. Stir.

GREEN BREEZE

makes 2 servings

1 handful fresh spinach

1 handful fresh parsley

½ pear

½ green apple

½ cucumber

2 stalks celery

1 slice papaya

½ inch fresh ginger, peeled

Juice spinach, parsley, pear, apple, cucumber, celery, papaya and ginger. Stir.

MEAN AND GREEN >

makes 2 servings

1 **green apple**
2 **stalks celery**
3 **leaves kale**
½ **cucumber**
½ **lemon, peeled**
1 **inch fresh ginger, peeled**
   Cucumber slices (optional)

Juice apple, celery, kale, cucumber, lemon and ginger. Stir. Garnish with cucumber slices.

COOL & CRISP

makes 2 servings

3 **stalks celery**
2 **apples**
1 **cup alfalfa sprouts**
   Ice cubes

Juice celery, apples and alfalfa sprouts. Stir. Serve over ice.

WALDORF JUICE >

makes 2 servings

2 **apples**

6 **leaves beet greens, Swiss chard or kale**

2 **stalks celery, plus additional for garnish**

Juice apples, beet greens and 2 stalks celery. Stir. Garnish with additional celery.

LEAN & GREEN

makes 2 servings

1 **cup chopped cabbage**

1 **cucumber**

1 **cup fresh parsley**

3 **spears asparagus**

1 **stalk celery**

1 **teaspoon lemon juice**

Juice cabbage, cucumber, parsley, asparagus and celery. Stir in lemon juice until well blended.

GREEN ENERGY >

makes 4 servings

2 **stalks celery**

2 **apples**

6 **leaves kale**

½ **cup fresh spinach**

½ **cucumber**

¼ **bulb fennel**

½ **lemon, peeled**

1 **inch fresh ginger, peeled**

Juice celery, apples, kale, spinach, cucumber, fennel, lemon and ginger. Stir.

ARTHRITIS TONIC

makes 2 servings

4 **spears asparagus**

3 **carrots**

3 **stalks celery**

1 **apple**

1 **cup broccoli florets**

1 **cup fresh parsley**

Juice asparagus, carrots, celery, apple, broccoli and parsley. Stir.

EASY BEING GREEN >

makes 2 servings

2 cups watercress

2 parsnips

2 stalks celery

½ cucumber

4 sprigs fresh basil

Juice watercress, parsnips, celery, cucumber and basil. Stir.

AFTERNOON SLUMP BUSTER

makes 2 servings

3 carrots

3 stalks celery

1 tomato

1 green onion

1 inch fresh ginger, peeled

½ clove garlic

Juice carrots, celery, tomato, green onion, ginger and garlic. Stir.

ORANGE

RED ORANGE JUICE

makes 2 servings

1 orange, peeled

1 apple

½ **cup raspberries, plus additional for garnish**

½ **cup strawberries**

Juice orange, apple, ½ cup raspberries and strawberries. Stir. Garnish with additional raspberries.

COLD AND FLU NINJA JUICE >

makes 1 serving

1 orange, peeled
½ lemon, peeled
⅛ small red onion
1 clove garlic
½ teaspoon honey

Juice orange, lemon, onion and garlic. Stir in honey until well blended.

ORANGE TRIPLE THREAT

makes 3 servings

8 carrots
1 mango, peeled
1 orange, peeled

Juice carrots, mango and orange. Stir.

INVIGORATING GREENS & CITRUS >

makes 2 servings

2 **oranges, peeled**
1 **grapefruit, peeled**
1 **zucchini**
½ **cup broccoli florets**
½ **inch fresh ginger, peeled**
   Orange slices (optional)

Juice oranges, grapefruit, zucchini, broccoli and ginger. Stir. Garnish with orange slices.

ORANGE BEET

makes 2 servings

2 **oranges, peeled**
1 **beet**

Juice oranges and beet. Stir.

VITAMIN BLAST >

makes 2 servings

¼ **cantaloupe, rind removed**

1 **orange, peeled**

¼ **papaya**

2 **leaves Swiss chard**

Cantaloupe cubes (optional)

Juice cantaloupe, orange, papaya and chard. Stir. Garnish with cantaloupe cubes.

KALE & FRUIT JUICE

makes 2 servings

2 **apples**

2 **carrots**

1 **orange, peeled**

1 **cup blackberries**

3 **leaves kale**

Juice apples, carrots, orange, blackberries and kale. Stir.

IMMUNITY BOOSTER >

makes 3 servings

1 **grapefruit, peeled**

2 **oranges, peeled**

½ **cup fresh blackberries**

Juice grapefruit, oranges and blackberries. Stir.

CITRUS TANG

makes 1 serving

1 **grapefruit, peeled**

1 **orange, peeled**

¼ **lemon, peeled**

¼ **lime, peeled**

Juice grapefruit, orange, lemon and lime. Stir.

CITRUS CARROT >

makes 2 servings

1 orange, peeled
2 carrots
½ lemon, peeled

Juice orange, carrots and lemon. Stir.

ORANGE RASPBERRY

makes 1 serving

2 oranges, peeled
12 raspberries

Juice oranges and raspberries. Stir.

ISLAND ORANGE JUICE >

makes 2 servings

2 **oranges, peeled**
2 **guavas**
½ **cup strawberries**

Juice oranges, guavas and strawberries. Stir.

MELON & ORANGE

makes 1 serving

½ **honeydew melon, peeled**
½ **cup cubed watermelon, rind removed**
½ **orange, peeled**

Juice honeydew, watermelon and orange. Stir.

CITRUS SPROUT >

makes 2 servings

1 cup Brussels sprouts

4 leaves romaine lettuce, plus additional for garnish

1 orange, peeled

½ apple

½ lemon, peeled

Juice Brussels sprouts, 4 romaine leaves, orange, apple and lemon. Stir. Garnish with additional romaine leaves.

DOUBLE MELON ORANGE

makes 2 servings

⅛ seedless watermelon, rind removed

⅛ cantaloupe, rind removed

1 orange, peeled

Juice watermelon, cantaloupe and orange. Stir.

MORNING BLEND >

makes 2 servings

¼ **pineapple, peeled**

1 **orange, peeled**

1 **inch fresh ginger, peeled**

Juice pineapple, orange and ginger. Stir.

WATERMELON ORANGE

makes 3 servings

¼ **seedless watermelon, rind removed**

2 **oranges, peeled**

   Ice cubes

Juice watermelon and oranges. Stir. Serve over ice.

SUPER C >

makes 3 servings

2 oranges, peeled
1 grapefruit, peeled
1 lemon, peeled
½ cup fresh cranberries
2 teaspoons honey

Juice oranges, grapefruit, lemon and cranberries. Stir in honey until blended.

SWISS ORANGE

makes 1 serving

2 oranges, peeled
3 leaves Swiss chard

Juice oranges and chard. Stir.

ORANGE APRICOT >

makes 2 servings

6 apricots
1 orange, peeled
  Ice cubes

Juice apricots and orange. Stir. Serve over ice.

PAPAYA POWER JUICE

makes 2 servings

¼ papaya
1 orange, peeled
¾ cup fresh parsley
1 clove garlic

Juice papaya, orange, parsley and garlic. Stir.

SWEET & SPICY CITRUS >

makes 2 servings

5 carrots
1 orange or 2 clementines, peeled
⅓ cup strawberries
1 lemon, peeled
½ inch fresh ginger, peeled
Strawberry slices (optional)

Juice carrots, orange, strawberries, lemon and ginger. Stir. Garnish with strawberry slices.

ORANGE BROCCOLI

makes 1 serving

2 oranges, peeled
1 cup broccoli

Juice oranges and broccoli. Stir.

PINEAPPLE

TROPICAL TWIST

makes 2 servings

⅛ **pineapple, peeled**

⅛ **seedless watermelon, rind removed**

1 **orange, peeled**

½ **mango, peeled**

⅓ **cup strawberries**

Mango wedges (optional)

Juice pineapple, watermelon, orange, mango and strawberries. Stir. Garnish with mango wedges.

TROPICAL FRUIT FLING >

makes 2 servings

Sugar (optional)
¼ pineapple, peeled
1 orange, peeled
½ mango, peeled
½ cup strawberries
½ cup coconut water

Rim glasses with sugar, if desired. Juice pineapple, orange, mango and strawberries. Stir in coconut water until well blended.

CABBAGE & PINEAPPLE

makes 1 serving

⅓ green cabbage
¼ pineapple, peeled
1 peach

Juice cabbage, pineapple and peach. Stir.

DOUBLE GREEN PINEAPPLE >

makes 1 serving

4 **leaves Swiss chard**

4 **leaves kale**

¼ **pineapple, peeled**

Juice chard, kale and pineapple. Stir.

MADRAS JUICE

makes 1 serving

⅛ **pineapple, peeled**

½ **cup cranberries**

6 **leaves collard greens**

½ **cucumber**

Juice pineapple, cranberries, greens and cucumber. Stir.

COOL CUCUMBER >

makes 2 servings

1 cucumber

¼ pineapple, peeled

¼ cup fresh cilantro

Pineapple wedges (optional)

Juice cucumber, pineapple and cilantro. Stir. Garnish with pineapple wedges.

PRUNEAPPLE

makes 2 servings

½ pineapple, peeled

2 plums

Juice pineapple and plums. Stir.

PURPLE PINEAPPLE JUICE >

makes 2 servings

1 **beet**
1 **pear**
¼ **pineapple, peeled**
1 **inch fresh ginger, peeled**

Juice beet, pear, pineapple and ginger. Stir.

PINEAPPLE EYE OPENER

makes 1 serving

¼ **pineapple, peeled**
½ **small onion**
1 **jalapeño pepper**
1 **teaspoon honey**

Juice pineapple, onion and jalapeño. Stir in honey until blended.

SPICY PINEAPPLE CARROT >

makes 2 servings

½ **pineapple, peeled**
2 **carrots**
1 **inch fresh ginger, peeled**
   Ice cubes

Juice pineapple, carrots and ginger. Stir. Serve over ice.

POPEYE'S FAVORITE JUICE

makes 1 serving

2 **cups fresh spinach**
¼ **pineapple, peeled**
1 **cup raspberries**

Juice spinach, pineapple and raspberries. Stir.

SWEET GREEN PINEAPPLE >

makes 1 serving

¼ **pineapple, peeled**
1 **cup broccoli florets**
1 **carrot**

Juice pineapple, broccoli and carrot. Stir.

TANGY PLUM

makes 2 servings

½ **pineapple, peeled**
2 **plums**
1 **grapefruit, peeled**

Juice pineapple, plums and grapefruit. Stir.

PINEAPPLE-MANGO-CUCUMBER >

makes 3 servings

¼ **pineapple, peeled**
1 **mango, peeled**
1 **cucumber**
½ **lemon, peeled**

Juice pineapple, mango, cucumber and lemon. Stir.

HONEY SPICE

makes 2 servings

1 **grapefruit, peeled**
¼ **pineapple, peeled**
½ **inch fresh ginger, peeled**
4 **whole cloves**
1 **teaspoon honey**

Juice grapefruit, pineapple and ginger. Stir. Pour into medium saucepan. Add cloves and honey; simmer over low heat until heated through. Remove from heat; set aside 5 minutes. Strain.

TROPICAL VEGGIE JUICE >

makes 2 servings

5 **leaves kale**
⅛ **pineapple, peeled**
½ **cucumber**
½ **cup coconut water**

Juice kale, pineapple and cucumber. Stir in coconut water until well blended.

PINEAPPLE CARROT

makes 1 serving

½ **fresh pineapple, peeled**
2 **carrots**

Juice pineapple and carrots. Stir.

RED CABBAGE & PINEAPPLE >

makes 2 servings

¼ **red cabbage**
¼ **pineapple, peeled**

Juice cabbage and pineapple. Stir.

HOTSY TOTSY

makes 2 servings

4 **carrots**
¼ **pineapple, peeled**
½ **lime, peeled**
¼ **small chile pepper**
2 **sprigs fresh cilantro**
  Ice cubes

Juice carrots, pineapple, lime, chile pepper and cilantro. Stir. Serve over ice.

JOINT COMFORT JUICE >

makes 2 servings

2 cups fresh spinach
¼ pineapple, peeled
1 pear
1 cup fresh parsley
½ grapefruit, peeled
   Sprigs fresh parsley (optional)

Juice spinach, pineapple, pear, parsley and grapefruit. Stir. Garnish with parsley sprigs.

PINEAPPLE FIZZ

makes 2 servings

½ pineapple, peeled
1 lemon, peeled
   Ice cubes
   Sparkling water

Juice pineapple and lemon. Stir. Serve over ice; top with sparkling water.

DRINK A RAINBOW

makes 6 servings

4 **carrots**

½ **pineapple, peeled**

2 **apples**

2 **pears**

1 **beet**

½ **cup Brussels sprouts**

½ **cup broccoli florets**

¼ **cup cauliflower florets**

Juice carrots, pineapple, apples, pears, beet, Brussels sprouts, broccoli and cauliflower. Stir.

ZIPPY APPLE PINEAPPLE

makes 1 serving

¼ **pineapple, peeled**

1 **apple**

½ **inch fresh ginger, peeled**

Juice pineapple, apple and ginger. Stir.

PINEAPPLE BERRY DELIGHT

makes 2 servings

½ **pineapple, peeled**
1 **cup fresh spinach**
½ **cup strawberries**
½ **cucumber**
 Ice cubes

Juice pineapple, spinach, strawberries and cucumber. Stir. Serve over ice.

STAR OF THE SHOW

makes 2 servings

2 **apricots**
2 **plums**
¼ **pineapple, peeled**
1 **peach**
1 **star fruit**

Juice apricots, plums, pineapple, peach and star fruit. Stir.

FRUIT NUTRITION CHART

FRUIT	CALORIES	TOTAL CARBOHYDRATE (g/%DV)	DIETARY FIBER (g/%DV)	SUGARS (g)
APPLE, medium (182g)	95	25g / 8%	4g / 17%	19g
APRICOT, small (35g)	15	17g / 1%	1g / 3%	3g
BANANA, medium (118g)	105	27g / 9%	3g / 12%	14g
BLACKBERRIES, 1 cup (144g)	62	15g / 5%	8g / 31%	7g
BLACKCURRANTS, 1 cup (112g)	71	17g / 6%	0g / 0%	0g
BLUEBERRIES, 1 cup (148g)	84	21g / 7%	4g / 14%	15g
CANTALOUPE, 1 wedge, medium (69g)	24	6g / 2%	1g / 2%	5g
CHERRIES, 1 cup (154g)	97	25g / 8%	3g / 13%	20g
CRANBERRIES, 1 cup (100g)	46	12g / 4%	5g / 18%	4g
GRAPEFRUIT, medium (246g)	52	13g / 4%	2g / 8%	9g
GRAPES, 1 cup (151g)	104	27g / 9%	1g / 5%	23g
GUAVA, medium (55g)	37	8g / 3%	3g / 12%	5g
HONEYDEW MELON, 1 medium wedge (125g)	45	11g / 4%	1g / 4%	10g
KIWI, medium (76g)	46	11g / 4%	2g / 9%	7g
LEMON, medium (108g)	22	12g / 4%	5g / 20%	0g
LIME, medium (67g)	20	7g / 2%	2g / 8%	1g
MANGO, medium (207g)	135	35g / 12%	4g / 15%	31g
ORANGE, medium (159g)	100	25g / 8%	7g / 29%	0g
PAPAYA, medium (304g)	119	30g / 10%	6g / 22%	18g
PEACH, medium (150g)	59	15g / 5%	2g / 9%	13g
PEAR, medium (178g)	103	28g / 9%	6g / 22%	17g
PINEAPPLE, thick slice (166g)	83	22g / 7%	2g / 9%	16g
PLUM, medium (66g)	30	8g / 3%	1g / 4%	7g
POMEGRANATE, medium (282g)	234	53g / 18%	11g / 45%	39g
RASPBERRIES, 1 cup (123g)	64	15g / 5%	8g / 32%	5g
STAR FRUIT, medium (91g)	28	6g / 2%	3g / 10%	4g
STRAWBERRIES, 1 cup (144g)	46	11g / 4%	3g / 12%	7g
TANGERINE, medium (88g)	47	12g / 4%	2g / 6%	9g
TOMATO, medium (123g)	22	5g / 2%	2g / 6%	3g
WATERMELON, 1 wedge, (286g)	86	22g / 7%	1g / 5%	18g

FRUIT NUTRITION CHART

PROTEIN (g/%DV)	SODIUM (mg)	VITAMIN A (%DV)	VITAMIN C (%DV)	VITAMIN E (%DV)	POTASSIUM (%DV)	FOLATE (%DV)	MAGNESIUM (%DV)	ZINC (%DV)
1g / 1%	2mg	2%	14%	2%	6%	1%	2%	0%
1g / 1%	0mg	13%	6%	2%	3%	1%	1%	0%
1g / 3%	1mg	2%	2%	1%	12%	6%	8%	1%
2g / 4%	1mg	6%	50%	8%	7%	9%	7%	5%
2g / 3%	2mg	5%	338%	6%	10%	0%	7%	2%
1g / 2%	2mg	2%	24%	4%	3%	2%	2%	2%
1g / 1%	11mg	47%	42%	0%	5%	4%	2%	1%
2g / 3%	0mg	2%	18%	1%	10%	2%	4%	1%
1g / 1%	2mg	1%	22%	6%	2%	0%	1%	1%
1g / 2%	0mg	28%	64%	1%	5%	4%	3%	1%
1g / 2%	3mg	2%	27%	1%	8%	1%	3%	1%
1g / 3%	1mg	7%	209%	2%	7%	7%	3%	1%
1g / 1%	23mg	1%	38%	0%	8%	6%	3%	1%
1g / 2%	2mg	1%	117%	6%	7%	5%	3%	1%
1g / 3%	3mg	1%	139%	0%	4%	0%	3%	1%
1g / 1%	1mg	1%	32%	1%	2%	1%	1%	0%
1g / 2%	4mg	32%	96%	12%	9%	7%	5%	1%
2g / 4%	3mg	8%	188%	0%	9%	12%	6%	1%
2g / 4%	9mg	67%	313%	11%	22%	29%	8%	1%
1g / 3%	0mg	10%	17%	5%	8%	1%	3%	2%
1g / 1%	2mg	1%	12%	1%	6%	3%	3%	1%
1g / 2%	2mg	2%	132%	0%	5%	7%	5%	1%
1g / 1%	0mg	5%	10%	1%	3%	1%	1%	0%
5g / 9%	9mg	0%	48%	8%	19%	27%	8%	7%
2g / 3%	1mg	1%	54%	5%	5%	6%	7%	3%
1g / 2%	2mg	1%	52%	1%	3%	3%	2%	1%
1g / 2%	1mg	0%	141%	2%	6%	9%	5%	1%
1g / 1%	2mg	12%	39%	1%	4%	4%	3%	0%
1g / 2%	6mg	20%	26%	3%	8%	5%	3%	1%
2g / 3%	3mg	33%	39%	1%	9%	2%	7%	2%

VEGETABLE NUTRITION CHART

VEGETABLE	CALORIES	TOTAL CARBOHYDRATE (g/%DV)	DIETARY FIBER (g/%DV)	SUGARS (g)
ARUGULA, ½ cup (10g)	3	0g / 0%	0.2g / 1%	0g
ASPARAGUS, 1 medium spear (16g)	3	1g / 0%	0.3g / 1%	0g
BEET, medium (82g)	35	8g / 3%	2g / 9%	6g
BEET GREENS, 1 cup (38g)	8	2g / 1%	1g / 6%	0g
BOK CHOY, 1 cup (76g)	12	3g / 1%	1g / 4%	1g
BROCCOLI, 1 cup (91g)	31	6g / 2%	2g / 9%	2g
BRUSSELS SPROUTS, 1 cup (88g)	38	8g / 3%	3g / 13%	2g
CABBAGE, ½ cup (35g)	8	2g / 1%	1g / 3%	0g
CARROT, medium (61g)	25	6g / 2%	2g / 7%	3g
CAULIFLOWER, 1 cup (100g)	25	5g / 2%	3g / 10%	2g
CELERY, 1 medium stalk (40g)	6	1g / 0%	1g / 3%	1g
COLLARD GREENS, 1 cup (36g)	11	2g / 1%	1g / 5%	0g
CUCUMBER, medium (301g)	45	11g / 4%	2g / 6%	5g
FENNEL, medium bulb (234g)	73	17g / 6%	7g / 29%	0g
JICAMA, medium (659g)	250	58g / 19%	32g / 129%	12g
KALE, 1 cup (67g)	34	7g / 2%	1g / 5%	0g
MUSTARD GREENS, 1 cup (56g)	15	3g / 1%	2g / 7%	1g
ONION, medium (110g)	44	10g / 3%	2g / 7%	5g
ONION, GREEN, 1 stalk (12g)	3	1g / 0%	0.4g / 2%	0g
PARSNIPS, 1 cup (133g)	100	24g / 8%	7g / 26%	4g
PEPPER, BELL, medium (119g)	24	6g / 2%	2g / 8%	3g
PEPPER, CHILE, medium (45g)	18	4g / 1%	1g / 3%	2g
PEPPER, JALAPEÑO, medium (14g)	4	1g / 0%	0g / 0%	1g
POTATO, medium (213g)	168	39g / 13%	3g / 11%	1g
POTATO, SWEET, medium (130g)	112	26g / 9%	4g / 16%	5g
RADICCHIO, 1 cup (40g)	9	2g / 1%	0.4g / 1%	0g
RADISHES, medium (4g)	1	0g / 0%	0g / 0%	0g
RHUBARB, 1 stalk (51g)	11	2g / 1%	1g / 4%	1g
ROMAINE LETTUCE, 1 cup (47g)	8	2g / 1%	1g / 4%	1g
SPINACH, 1 cup (30g)	7	1g / 0%	1g / 3%	0g
SQUASH, BUTTERNUT, 1 cup (140g)	63	16g / 5%	3g / 11%	3g
SQUASH, ZUCCHINI, 1 cup (124g)	20	4g / 1%	1g / 5%	2g
SWISS CHARD, 1 cup (36g)	7	1g / 0%	1g / 2%	0g
WATERCRESS, 1 cup (34g)	4	0g / 0%	0g / 0%	0g

VEGETABLE NUTRITION CHART

PROTEIN (g/%DV)	SODIUM (mg)	VITAMIN A (%DV)	VITAMIN C (%DV)	VITAMIN E (%DV)	POTASSIUM (%DV)	FOLATE (%DV)	MAGNESIUM (%DV)	ZINC (%DV)
0.3g / 1%	3mg	5%	2%	0%	1%	2%	1%	0%
0.4g / 1%	0mg	2%	1%	1%	1%	2%	1%	1%
1g / 3%	64mg	1%	7%	0%	8%	22%	5%	2%
1g / 2%	86mg	48%	19%	3%	8%	1%	7%	1%
1g / 2%	7mg	5%	34%	0%	5%	15%	10%	1%
3g / 5%	30mg	11%	135%	4%	8%	14%	5%	2%
3g / 6%	22mg	13%	125%	4%	10%	13%	5%	2%
0.4g / 1%	6mg	1%	24%	0%	2%	5%	1%	0%
1g / 1%	42mg	204%	6%	2%	6%	3%	2%	1%
2g / 4%	30mg	0%	77%	0%	9%	14%	4%	2%
0.3g / 1%	32mg	4%	2%	1%	3%	4%	1%	0%
1g / 2%	7mg	48%	21%	4%	2%	15%	1%	0%
2g / 4%	6mg	6%	14%	0%	13%	5%	10%	4%
3g / 6%	122mg	6%	47%	0%	28%	16%	10%	3%
5g / 9%	26mg	3%	222%	15%	28%	20%	20%	7%
2g / 4%	29mg	206%	134%	0%	9%	5%	6%	2%
2g / 3%	14mg	118%	65%	6%	6%	26%	4%	1%
1g / 2%	4mg	0%	14%	0%	5%	5%	3%	1%
0g / 0%	1mg	10%	9%	0%	1%	0%	1%	0%
2g / 3%	13mg	0%	38%	10%	14%	22%	10%	5%
1g / 2%	4mg	9%	159%	2%	6%	3%	3%	1%
1g / 2%	3mg	11%	182%	2%	4%	3%	3%	1%
0g / 0%	0mg	2%	10%	0%	1%	2%	1%	0%
5g / 9%	11mg	0%	20%	0%	25%	7%	12%	4%
2g / 4%	72mg	369%	5%	2%	13%	4%	8%	3%
1g / 1%	9mg	0%	5%	5%	3%	6%	1%	2%
0g / 0%	2mg	0%	1%	0%	0%	0%	0%	0%
1g / 1%	2mg	1%	7%	1%	4%	1%	2%	0%
1g / 1%	4mg	82%	19%	0%	3%	16%	2%	1%
1g / 2%	24mg	56%	14%	3%	5%	15%	6%	1%
1g / 3%	6mg	298%	49%	10%	14%	9%	12%	1%
2g / 3%	12mg	5%	35%	1%	9%	9%	5%	2%
1g / 1%	77mg	44%	18%	3%	4%	1%	7%	1%
1g / 2%	14mg	22%	24%	2%	3%	1%	2%	0%

INDEX

INDEX

METRIC CONVERSION CHART

VOLUME MEASUREMENTS (dry)

$^1/_8$ teaspoon = 0.5 mL
$^1/_4$ teaspoon = 1 mL
$^1/_2$ teaspoon = 2 mL
$^3/_4$ teaspoon = 4 mL
1 teaspoon = 5 mL
1 tablespoon = 15 mL
2 tablespoons = 30 mL
$^1/_4$ cup = 60 mL
$^1/_3$ cup = 75 mL
$^1/_2$ cup = 125 mL
$^2/_3$ cup = 150 mL
$^3/_4$ cup = 175 mL
1 cup = 250 mL
2 cups = 1 pint = 500 mL
3 cups = 750 mL
4 cups = 1 quart = 1 L

VOLUME MEASUREMENTS (fluid)

1 fluid ounce (2 tablespoons) = 30 mL
4 fluid ounces ($^1/_2$ cup) = 125 mL
8 fluid ounces (1 cup) = 250 mL
12 fluid ounces (1$^1/_2$ cups) = 375 mL
16 fluid ounces (2 cups) = 500 mL

WEIGHTS (mass)

$^1/_2$ ounce = 15 g
1 ounce = 30 g
3 ounces = 90 g
4 ounces = 120 g
8 ounces = 225 g
10 ounces = 285 g
12 ounces = 360 g
16 ounces = 1 pound = 450 g

DIMENSIONS

$^1/_{16}$ inch = 2 mm
$^1/_8$ inch = 3 mm
$^1/_4$ inch = 6 mm
$^1/_2$ inch = 1.5 cm
$^3/_4$ inch = 2 cm
1 inch = 2.5 cm

OVEN TEMPERATURES

250°F = 120°C
275°F = 140°C
300°F = 150°C
325°F = 160°C
350°F = 180°C
375°F = 190°C
400°F = 200°C
425°F = 220°C
450°F = 230°C

BAKING PAN SIZES

Utensil	Size in Inches/Quarts	Metric Volume	Size in Centimeters
Baking or Cake Pan (square or rectangular)	8 × 8 × 2	2 L	20 × 20 × 5
	9 × 9 × 2	2.5 L	23 × 23 × 5
	12 × 8 × 2	3 L	30 × 20 × 5
	13 × 9 × 2	3.5 L	33 × 23 × 5
Loaf Pan	8 × 4 × 3	1.5 L	20 × 10 × 7
	9 × 5 × 3	2 L	23 × 13 × 7
Round Layer Cake Pan	8 × 1½	1.2 L	20 × 4
	9 × 1½	1.5 L	23 × 4
Pie Plate	8 × 1¼	750 mL	20 × 3
	9 × 1¼	1 L	23 × 3
Baking Dish or Casserole	1 quart	1 L	—
	1½ quart	1.5 L	—
	2 quart	2 L	—